Why Don't Ships
by Jillian Powell

Contents

Section 1

Why Do Animals Hibernate?   2

Why Do Some Trees Lose Their Leaves in Winter?   5

Why Don't Ships Sink?   7

Why Don't Aeroplanes Fall Out of the Sky?   9

Section 2

What is Cloning?   11

What is the Ozone Hole?   16

What is Global Warming?   20

Section 3

How Does the Internet Work?   24

How Do Birds Fly?   28

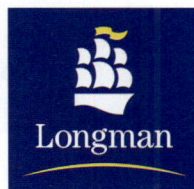

Longman

Edinburgh Gate
Harlow, Essex

Why Do Animals Hibernate?

When Do Animals Hibernate?

In autumn, the weather gets colder and the days get shorter. Some animals get ready to hibernate. Small animals like dormice and hedgehogs hibernate. Some bats and birds and insects hibernate. In winter, it can be very cold and there can be frost or snow on the ground so it is hard for animals to stay warm and find food to eat. They hibernate to stay safe in the cold winter months.

Getting Ready to Hibernate

Animals get ready to hibernate by eating lots of food so their bodies put on fat quickly. The fat helps them stay warm in the winter. They look for a warm place to sleep which is safe from their enemies. Some animals make nests in tree roots or in burrows under the ground. They may have to travel a long way to find a safe place to hibernate. Some bats and insects fly hundreds of kilometres to find caves to hibernate in.

Animals eat lots before hibernating: the extra fat helps keep them warm.

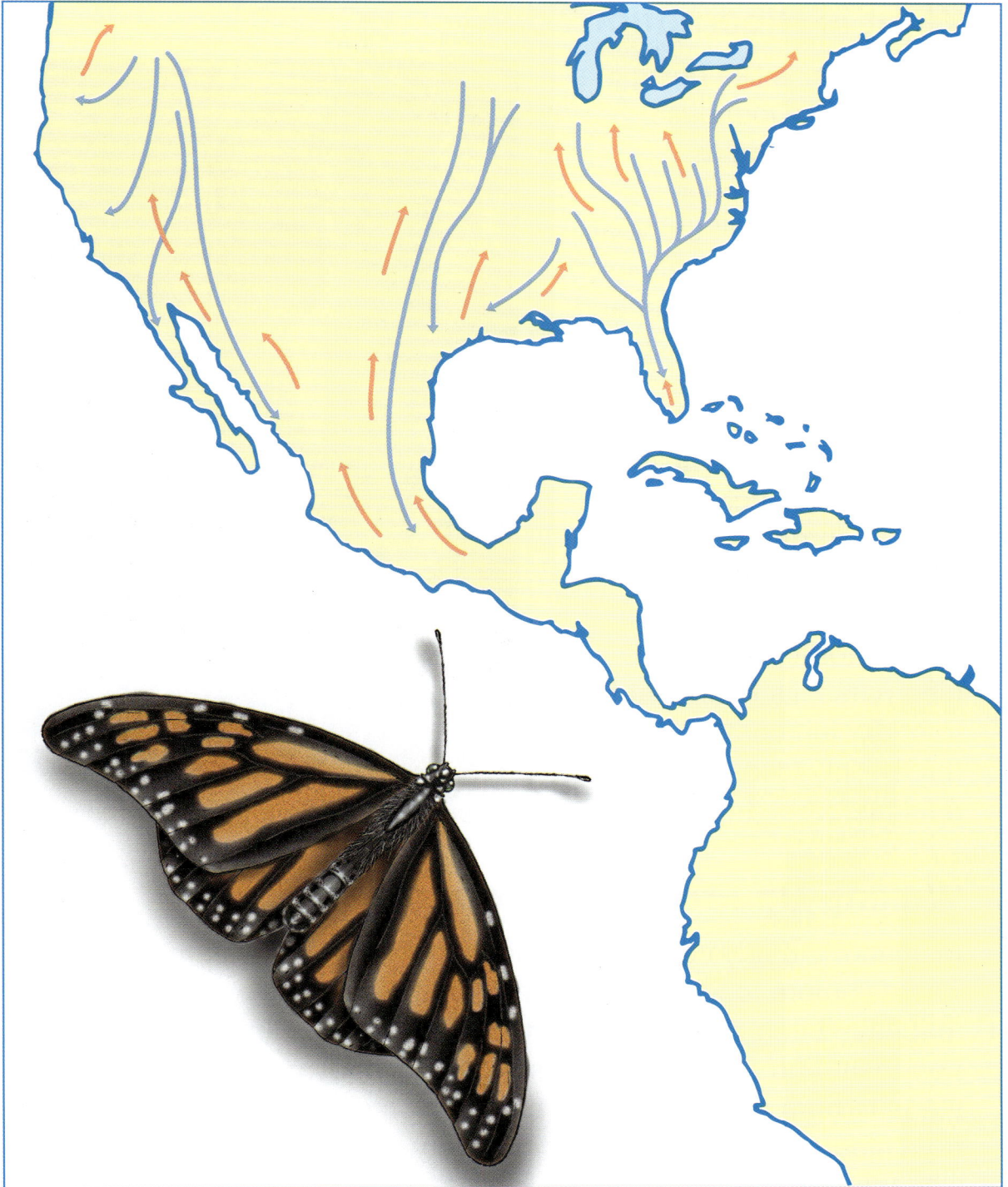

Monarch butterflies migrate south to hibernate.

What is Hibernation?

Hibernation is like being in a deep sleep. Dormouse means "sleep mouse" because a dormouse hibernates for half the year. The animal's body gets much colder and its heartbeat and breathing slow down. Its body temperature can fall from 37 °C to 2 °C. This saves energy. The animal is just warm enough to stay alive. A dormouse's heart beats up to two hundred times a minute when it is looking for food. When it hibernates, its heartbeat falls to under ten beats a minute. It may only take one breath a minute.

A dormouse hibernates for half the year.

Waking Up From Hibernation

In spring, the days get longer and the ground gets warmer. There is more food for wild animals and birds to eat. Animals that have been hibernating start to wake up. The animal's heartbeat and breathing get faster and its body gets warmer. It starts to burn up fat to use as energy. Some animals wake up from hibernation at the same time every year. Others wake up when the weather starts to get warmer.

Why Do Some Trees Lose Their Leaves in Winter?

Evergreen Trees

Evergreen trees stay green all through the year. They grow tough leaves or hard needles that can live through the cold winter. As their old leaves fall, they grow new ones so they are never bare.

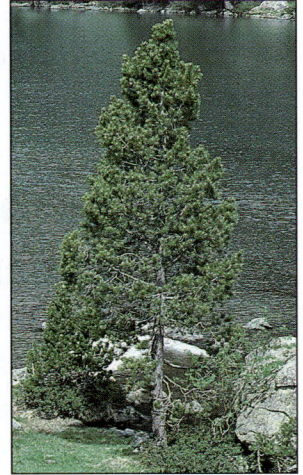

Deciduous Trees

Trees that lose their leaves in winter are called **deciduous** trees. Deciduous trees lose all their leaves in autumn so they are bare for part of the year. They grow in the parts of the world which have four seasons. In spring, deciduous trees grow new leaves. In summer, they grow flowers. In autumn they form seeds to make new plants. Then they lose their leaves so they can rest through the cold winter months when there is not enough sun and rain to help them grow.

Evergreen trees in winter and summer.

Deciduous trees in winter and summer.

Using Energy

Trees use up energy growing and losing leaves. Leaves need sun and rain so they can grow and make food for trees. They do this by **photosynthesis**, which means "putting together by light". A green chemical in the leaves traps energy from the sunlight. The leaves use this energy to put together carbon dioxide from the air and water from rain to make sugars which feed the tree.

How Leaves Fall

In autumn, as the days get shorter and colder, the green chemical in leaves begins to break down. The yellow, red and orange chemicals left in the leaves give the trees their bright autumn colours. Soon the ground becomes too cold for trees to take up enough water. A layer of cork grows across the leaf stalk so the leaf dies back and falls. Most trees lose their leaves in autumn but some trees, such as the beech, keep their old leaves until the spring. The new leaves will start to grow when there is enough sun and rain in the spring.

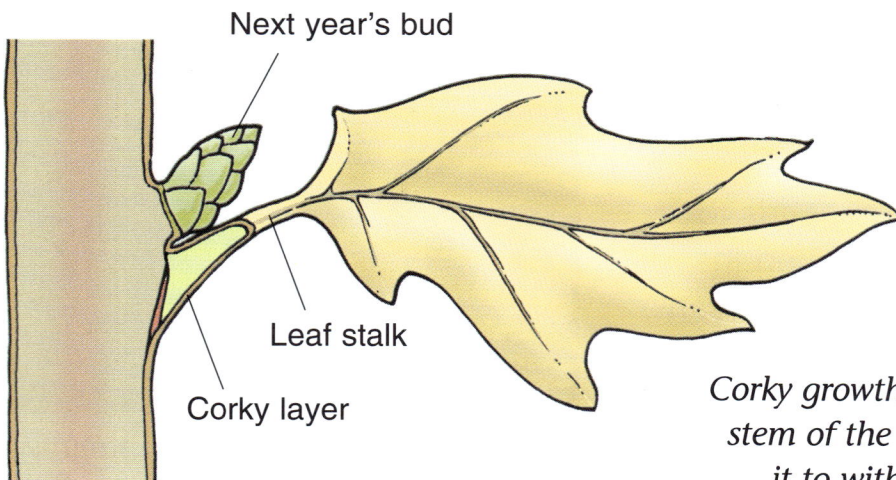

Next year's bud

Leaf stalk

Corky layer

Corky growth across the stem of the leaf causes it to wither and die.

Why Don't Ships Sink?

To Float or To Sink?

Some objects can float on water, but others sink. A huge ship can float but a small object such as a marble sinks. It is not the size or the weight of an object which makes it float or sink. It is the object's shape and its density. A cork floats on water because cork is less dense than water. A marble sinks in water because it is made of glass which is more dense than water. Objects float when their density is less than the water around them.

A huge passenger ship looks like a floating city.

Shipbuilding Materials

Ships and boats can be made of steel, iron, wood or fibreglass. Wood and fibreglass are light materials that float easily but steel and iron are dense and heavy. A giant cruise liner can weigh as much as a big building. Ships have to be built in a special way so they can float even when they are very heavy.

How Ships Float

When a ship floats, it is pushing water aside. The water around the ship pushes back. This is the **force** of the water. The force of the water pushing back must be the same as the weight of the ship. A heavy ship needs to push aside lots of water so it is built with a wide and hollow hull. A hollow hull is lighter than a solid one but it can still push lots of water aside. Heavy ships are built with high sides so lots of water can push up against them and keep them afloat.

When a ship has a heavy cargo, it must be loaded on board carefully so the ship sits evenly in the water. Cargo ships have a line marked around them called the **Plimsoll Line**. This shows how low the ship is floating in the water, and how much cargo can be safely loaded on board.

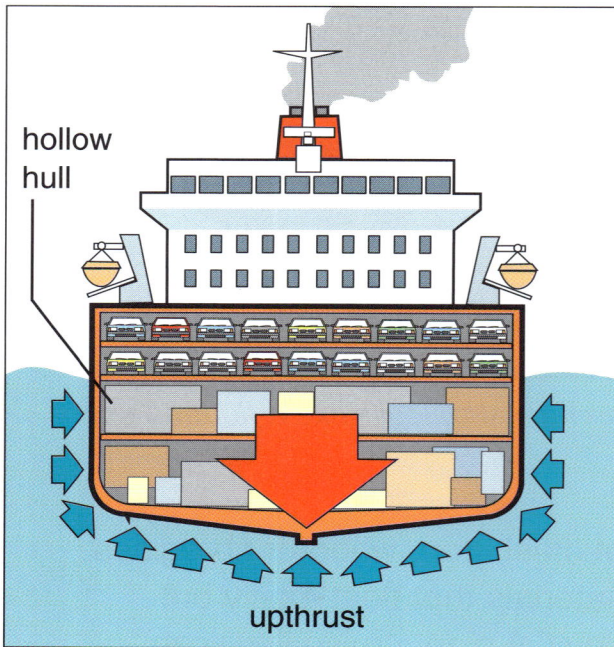

hollow hull

upthrust

The hull of a ship pushes water aside, and the force of the water pushes back.

The white Plimsoll Line shows how low the ship is floating.

Why Don't Aeroplanes Fall Out of the Sky?

Overcoming Gravity

Aeroplanes are very heavy. They are pulled down by their own weight and by gravity. Gravity is the force that pulls everything down to the Earth. An aeroplane must be built in a special way so it can climb into the air and stay there while it flies. It must be able to overcome its weight and the force of gravity to stay in the air.

Wing Design

An aircraft needs wings to be able to fly. The wings have a special shape. They are curved on top. This means that the air flowing over the wings has to travel further than the air flowing underneath them. The air above has to move faster to keep up so it travels faster than the air underneath the wings. Air that moves fast has a lower pressure. The air moving underneath the wings is moving slower, so it has a higher pressure that lifts the wings up. The aeroplane stays in the air because the air flowing over its wings gives it a lift which is greater than its weight.

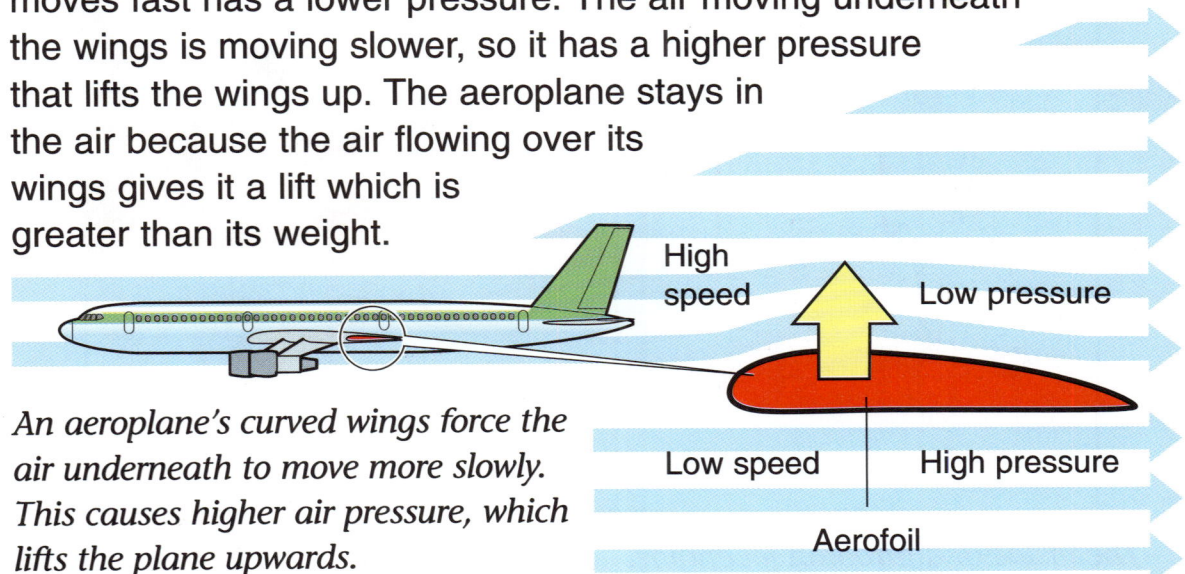

An aeroplane's curved wings force the air underneath to move more slowly. This causes higher air pressure, which lifts the plane upwards.

High speed

Low pressure

Low speed

High pressure

Aerofoil

Air Drag

Air must be able to flow over and under the plane smoothly. Aeroplanes are built so air can flow easily around them. When an aeroplane is flying, it is pushing air out of its way. The air pushes back against the aeroplane and slows it down. This is the force of the air. It is called **drag**.

Aeroplanes overcome the drag of the air by the power of their jet engines. Jet engines suck in air at one end. The air is heated by the aircraft fuel so it gets hotter and the air pressure rises. The hot air shoots out of the exhaust very quickly, pushing the aeroplane forward. Air is forced over and under the wings. The plane is lifted while it flies.

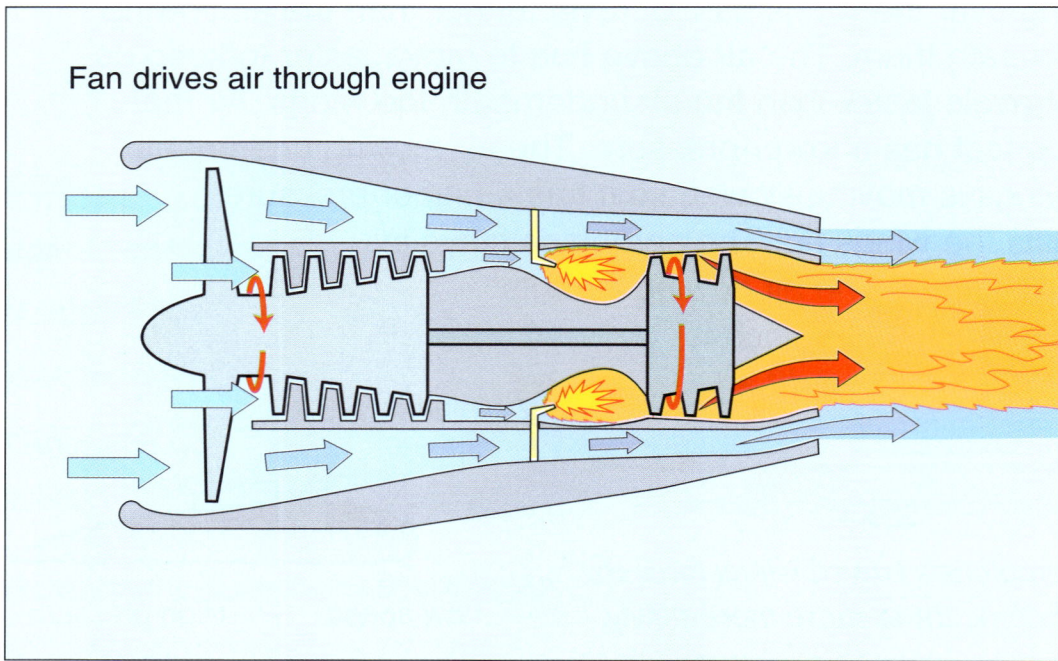

Fan drives air through engine

The inside of a turbofan jet engine.

What is Cloning?

Clones are exact copies of living plants or animals. Scientists have found out how to make clones or copies of living things by copying their cells. Plants and animals are all made up from small units called cells. Each cell has a nucleus at its centre with a jelly-like stuff around the outside. The nucleus is the control centre of the cell. Inside the nucleus are lots of tiny strings called **chromosomes**. These chromosomes are made from thousands of genes.

You can see the chromosomes coloured green in the cell's neucleus.

Genes

Scientists are still learning about genes. They know that genes are made from an acid called DNA. DNA acts like a special code that the cells in our bodies use. Cells follow this code to make proteins. Each protein does something different, such as giving us the colour of our eyes or our hair.

We all have different genes which we get from our parents. Our genes control our features, our height and the colour of our skin and hair. To make an exact copy of any living person, animal or plant, scientists have to copy its genes exactly. This is what they have learned to do by cloning.

What have you inherited from your mum and dad?

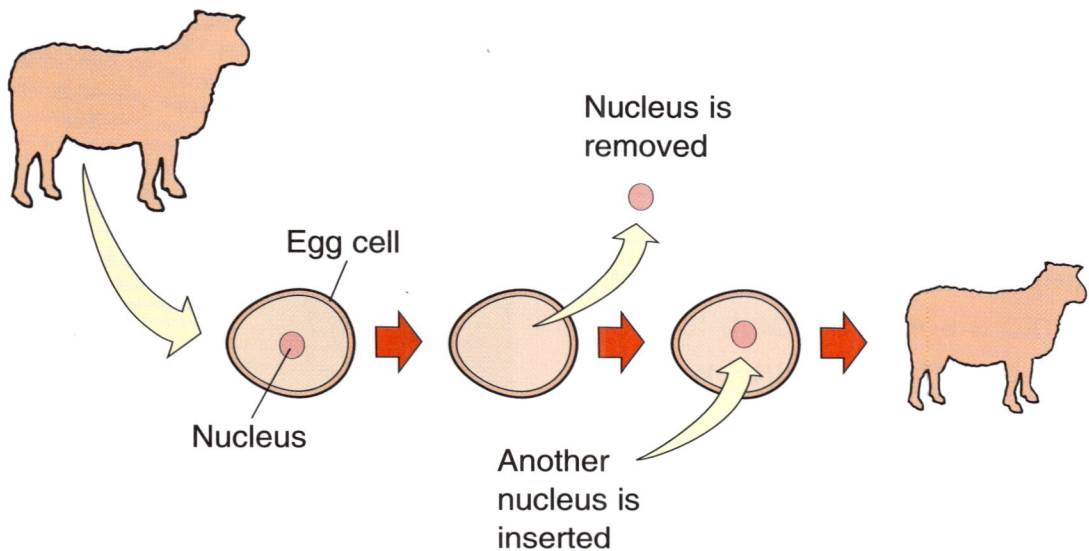

Basic cell stages in cloning.

Labels in diagram: Nucleus is removed, Egg cell, Nucleus, Another nucleus is inserted

Cloning Plants and Animals

Plants can be cloned by taking a cutting from a stem or leaf of the parent plant. The cutting will grow on in soil to form a new plant. Scientists found that they were able to clone plants by using just one cell from the parent plant. They then began to look for ways to clone animals.

Scientists began to study cloning because they wanted to be able to copy or clone the best plants and animals, such as the cows that make the most milk or the sheep that make most wool. They found a way to clone an animal using just two cells. One must be an egg cell taken from the mother animal. Scientists take out the nucleus of the egg cell and put back the nucleus from another cell in the animal's body. This means that a baby can be made by using two of the mother's cells without any father. It will be an exact copy or clone of its mother.

Dolly the Sheep

In l996 scientists cloned a sheep which they called Dolly. They took an egg cell from one sheep and took out its nucleus. They then put back a nucleus taken from another sheep's udder. The egg cell was put into a sheep's womb to grow into a baby lamb. In this way, a whole flock of sheep could be cloned from just one mother.

Dolly the Sheep, an exact copy of her mum.

She looks exactly like any other sheep. But the cloning method used to produce Dolly may change our lives

By Roger Highfield, Science Editor

THE possibility that an adult human can be cloned from a single blood or skin cell was raised yesterday with the announcement that scientists have produced the world's first clone of an adult animal.

The clone, a Finn Dorset sheep called Dolly, paves the way to unprecedented genetic manipulation of farmyard animals, more cheaply and more accurately than ever before.

A single cell could be taken from a prize bull, elite racehorse, or award-winning pig, and hundreds of identical animals produced using the patented cloning technology developed at the Roslin Institute and PPL Therapeutics, near Edinburgh.

Introduction or deletion of genes in the cloned cells also offers the means to make animals that produce drugs in their milk, grow faster for meat production, or are resistant to diseases such as scrapie and BSE.

The first sheep altered using this method may be born later this year, though it will be several years before scientists will have developed the means to alter many genes simultaneously, which will be necessary to boost growth or make leaner beef.

But any other use of the technology, for instance to mass-produce human eggs for use in in-vitro fertilisation, is outlawed, said Dr Ron James, managing director of PPL.

The world starts to think …

14

Cloning People

Scientists could use the same method to clone humans. They could take the genes from one body cell and put them in the mother's egg cell to make a clone. Clones could be made as spare copies of people to provide parts needed for surgery. Scientists could also help people who cannot have children by making clone babies.

Cloned people would look like the person who gave the cells but they would be different people in the same way that identical twins are different. This is because the way we are brought up makes us all different people.

The science of cloning is moving fast but some people think it is wrong to clone animals and humans. They think it is going against Nature and that there may be hidden dangers.

Cloning for human babies must never happen, says poll

By Roger Highfield, Science Editor

HUMAN cloning for reproductive purposes should never be allowed, according to public opinion noted in a study published yesterday.

Those taking part in the survey of attitudes, organised in response to a government consultation exercise, were almost unanimous in their abhorrence of the technique of reproduction without men.

They were "shocked by the implications". However, some felt that it was inevitable.

The 79 people interviewed for the survey, by NOP and Research Business International for the Wellcome Trust, were initially prepared to support cloning to create tissue and organs for medical treatments.

Later, having thought about how it involved the destruction of human embryos, they expressed reservations and caveats on the type and use of the research.

The study found a lack of trust in scientists and those in control of research, and faith in an *X Files* view of people being kept in the dark.

And what do you think …?

15

What is the Ozone Hole?

Ozone is a layer of gas in the Earth's atmosphere. It lies between twelve and forty kilometres above the Earth's surface. It is only a tiny part of the atmosphere but there would be no life on Earth without it. It keeps us safe from the Sun's dangerous ultraviolet rays which can cause sunburn and damage living things.

In 1985, scientists found a hole in the ozone layer over the Antarctic. It is not a real hole, but scientists call it a hole when half or more of the ozone is destroyed. We cannot see the ozone hole. Scientists need equipment such as satellites to see it. The ozone layer is being destroyed by human-made chemicals. The hole is caused mainly by chemicals called **CFCs**, which are chlorofluorocarbons.

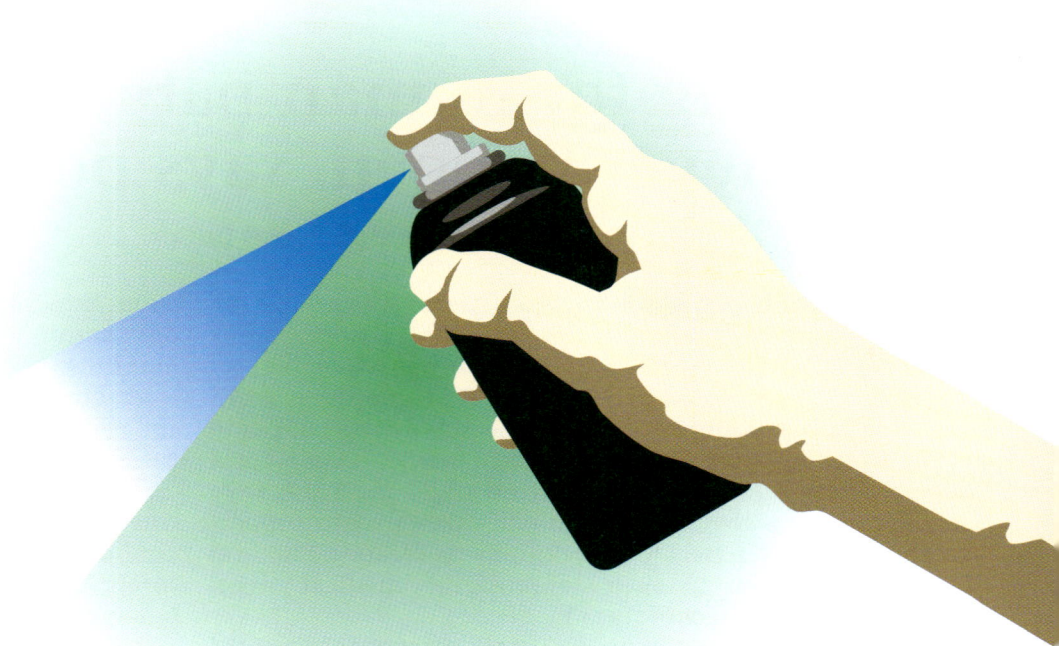

CFCs are now banned in aerosols.

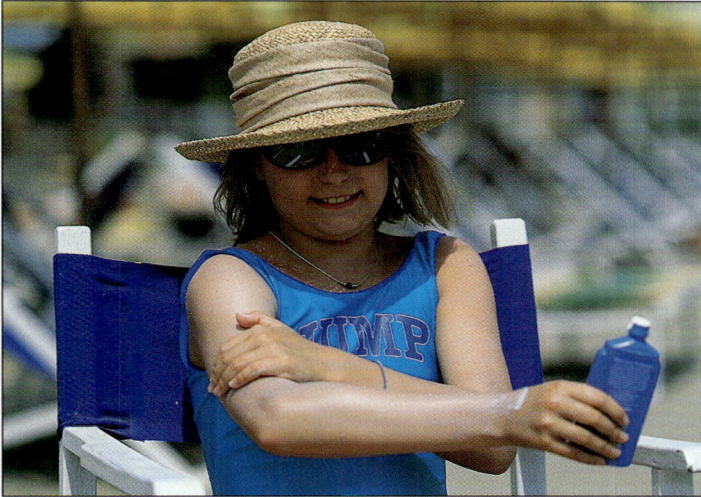

It is important to protect your skin and eyes from ultraviolet light.

CFCs

CFCs were invented in 1928. They were used in air conditioning units, fridges, fast food packaging and aerosols. They are now banned in many countries but they are still being used in some parts of the world. When CFCs are broken down by sunlight, they release carbon atoms. These atoms attack and destroy ozone. Other chemicals that destroy ozone are still being used in factories and in products such as pesticides.

Ultraviolet Light

Ozone is now being destroyed across the world. This means that the Sun's harmful ultraviolet rays can reach the Earth more easily. People and plants need some ultraviolet light to live, but too much ultraviolet can harm living things. Ultraviolet rays can burn our skin and cause skin diseases such as skin cancer. They can harm our eyes too. Scientists think they may also make our immune systems weaker, which means we cannot fight diseases so well. Ultraviolet rays can also damage or kill plants, such as plankton, the tiny plants and animals found in the oceans that fish feed on.

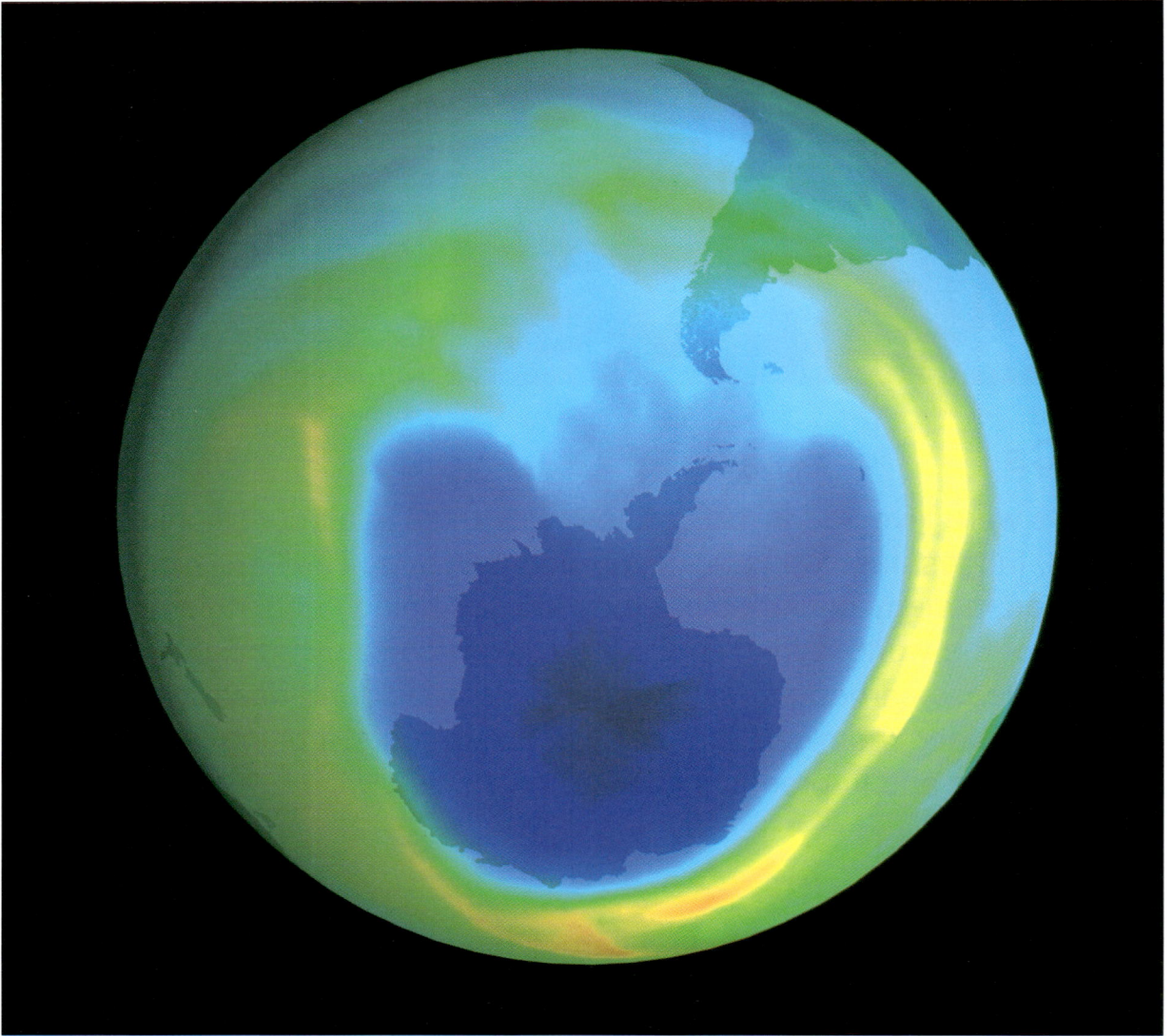

A satellite picture of the ozone hole over Antarctica.

Reducing the Ozone Hole

The size of the ozone hole changes from year to year. Scientists use satellites to track and measure the ozone hole. They are trying to find ways to stop ozone being destroyed, such as using laser beams to destroy CFCs. Countries must work together to try to repair the damage and stop more of the ozone layer being destroyed in the future.

What is Global Warming?

As the Sun's heat reaches the Earth, some of it is taken in by plants, trees and the oceans. Some of it bounces back into the atmosphere. Carbon dioxide in the air can trap the Sun's heat, warming up the Earth. Carbon dioxide and other gases that trap the Sun's heat are called **greenhouse gases**. They make the Earth's atmosphere work like a greenhouse by trapping the Sun's heat just like glass does in a greenhouse.

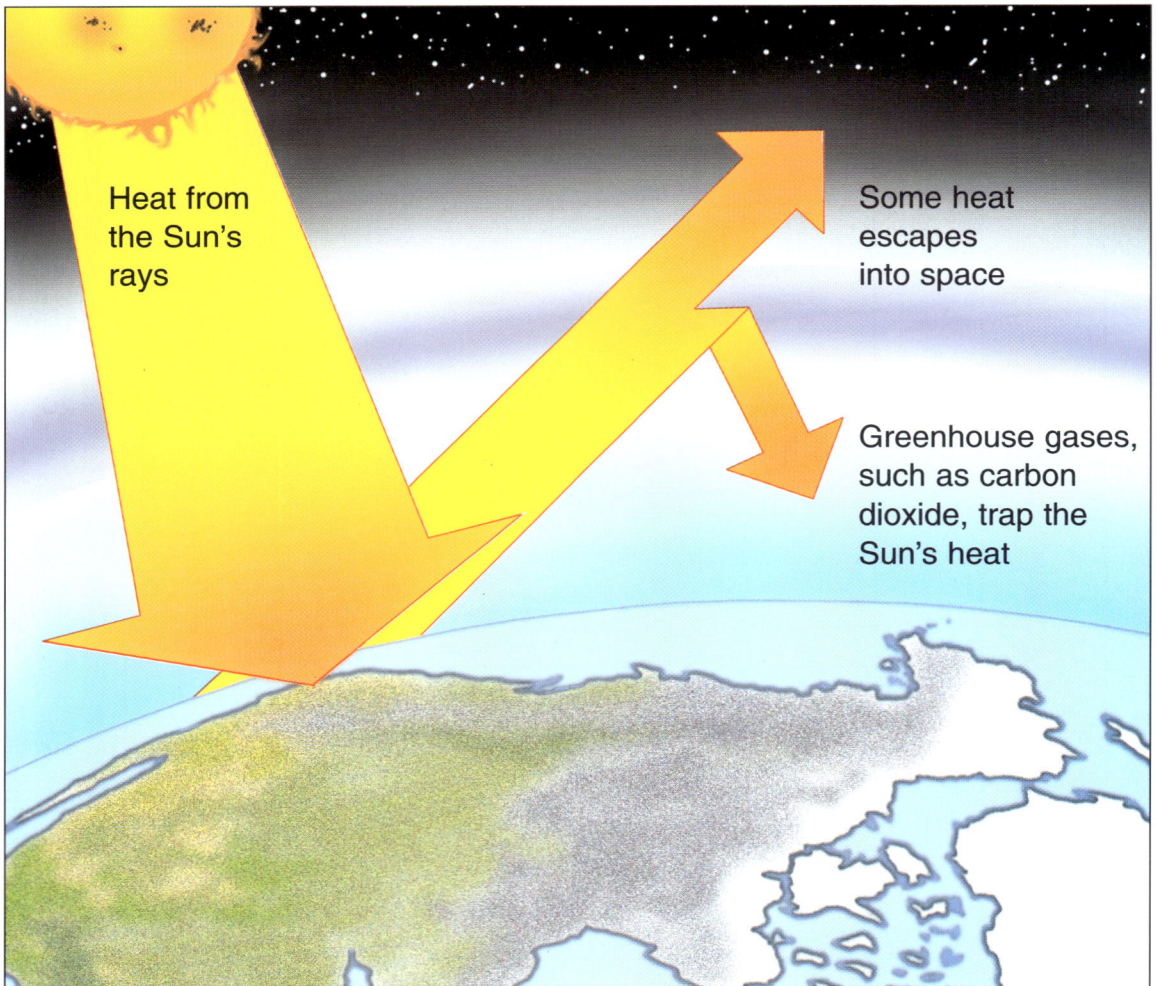

Heat from the Sun's rays

Some heat escapes into space

Greenhouse gases, such as carbon dioxide, trap the Sun's heat

The greenhouse effect: the Sun's rays are reflected back to the Earth.

How Carbon Dioxide is Made

Carbon dioxide is made when we burn fossil fuels such as oil, coal and gas. These natural fuels contain carbon. When they are burned, the carbon goes into the air as carbon dioxide. The more carbon dioxide there is in the air, the warmer the Earth becomes. Carbon dioxide is being made all the time by factories and by transport like cars and aeroplanes. Some carbon dioxide is taken in by trees and plants as they grow. But in the last century, so much fuel was burned and so many forests and trees were cut down, that the amount of carbon dioxide has increased.

Forests being destroyed to make way for farming.

Global Warming in the Future

The greenhouse effect means that the Earth's atmosphere is warming up. This is called **global warming**. Global warming will change the Earth and life on it. Scientists think that the Earth could warm up by about 4°C in about 150 years. If this happens, frozen water in glaciers and in the ice caps around the North and South Poles could melt. This will make sea levels rise, flooding low lands. Whole countries could disappear under the seas. Global warming will also cause more storms, and extremes of weather like droughts and hurricanes. It will be harder for farmers to grow enough crops to feed the world.

Natural disasters are occurring more frequently as the Earth's climate changes.

What Needs to Be Done?

Most experts now agree that we need to take action to reduce the amount of carbon dioxide in the Earth's atmosphere. We know that in time fossil fuels such as oil and coal will run out and we should develop clean forms of energy such as sun, wind and wave power. We need to reduce the number of cars on the roads or find new ways to power them. A third way of reducing carbon dioxide is to plant more trees and stop rainforests being cut down and destroyed.

How Does the Internet Work?

The Internet is a huge network of computers. It has no control centre. It is made up of millions of computers linked together by telephone lines around the world. If a computer is plugged into a telephone line, it can receive information from other computers and send information to them.

History of the Internet

The Internet was invented in the United States in the 1960s. The US government wanted to find ways of sending information around the country even if part of the computer system was destroyed by war or nuclear attack. They found a way of linking computers together without a control centre, to make the network bomb-proof. The first network was built in 1969 linking together four universities. The network grew so that by the 1970s it was worldwide.

Who Owns the Internet?

The computers and cables that make up the Internet are owned by people and organisations, but no-one owns the Internet. No-one knows how many people or how many computers there are on the Internet. Some experts think that about 5% of the world's population, or 300 million people around the world are using the Internet but the number is growing all the time.

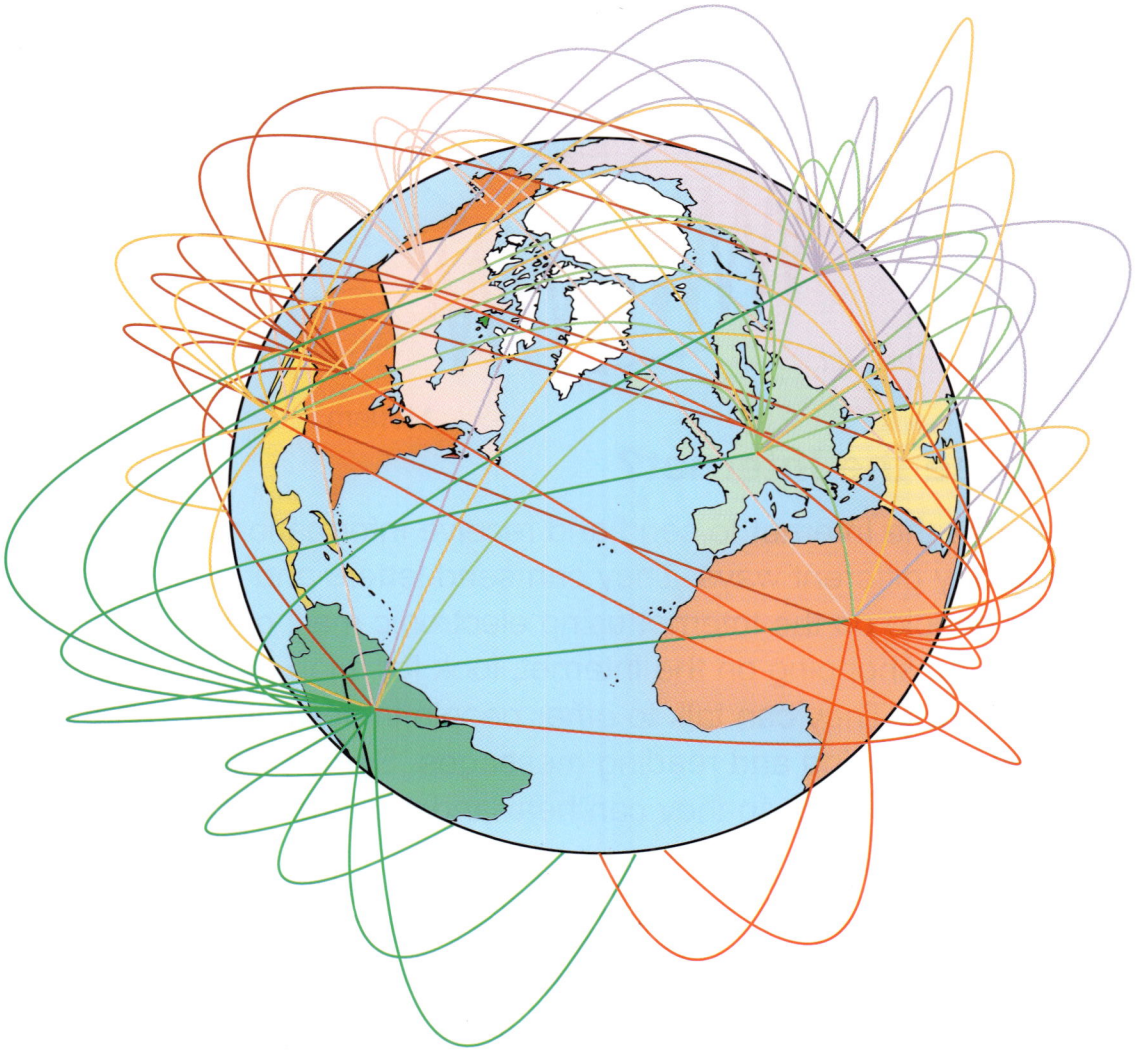

The Internet connects computers
all around the world.

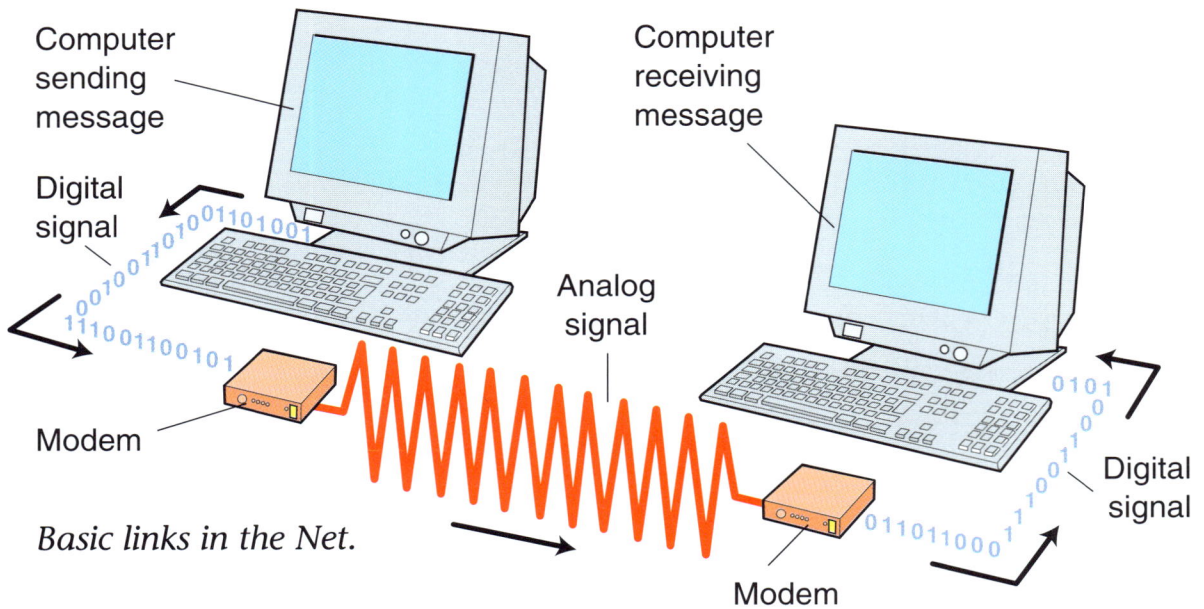

Computer sending message

Computer receiving message

Digital signal

00100110100 1001101001

111001100101

Analog signal

Modem

0101 1 0 0 1 1 0 0 1 1

Digital signal

Basic links in the Net.

011011000 1

Modem

Why Use the Internet?

People use the Internet to send and receive information. They do this in many different ways. They can send letters and other files to other people on the Internet using electronic mail, or e-mail. They can go shopping on the Internet, look for a job, or catch up with the news. They can talk to other people in newsgroups and chatrooms by typing and reading messages. Some people have audio and video links so they can hear and see each other.

The WWW

The most famous part of the Internet is the worldwide web (WWW). This is the multimedia part of the Internet. It is made up of millions of web pages which can contain video and audio material as well as text and pictures. Anyone who is connected up to the Internet can make their own web page that others can read. There are so many web pages on the worldwide web that people have to use search engines to find information they need. These are powerful engines that can sort and find information from millions of pages.

Connecting to the Internet

Most of the computers on the Internet are in people's homes or in offices or schools. People connect up to the Internet when they need to. They dial a number to connect up to one of the big host or server computers. When the connection is made, they are able to surf the Internet. There are also powerful computers in universities, government offices and large companies. These computers are connected up to the Internet all the time.

Computers send and receive data through a **modem**. A modem allows computers to talk to one another across ordinary telephone lines. It turns digital signals from the computer into analog signals that can be sent down a telephone line. At the other end, another modem turns the analog signals back into digital signals so they can be received on a computer. Modems work at different speeds. These speeds are measured in bits per second. This shows how fast information and e-mail can be sent and received.

Computer data can also be sent along high speed cable and through satellite links. The cables which send data across the Internet are made from strands of glass. They use pulses of light to send information. Information can travel thousands of times faster than along ordinary telephone lines. Telephone lines are now being replaced with cable and satellite links so the Internet can work faster.

More people use the Internet every day.

How Do Birds Fly?

A Bird's Body

The only animals that can fly are birds, insects and bats. Birds are the largest, fastest and strongest flyers of all. Their bodies are made for flying. They are light but strong. Flight uses lots of energy so a bird's body turns food into energy very quickly. Its heartbeat is very fast. It beats up to fifteen times a second so it can carry blood quickly round the body to give energy. Their wings are strong enough to lift and hold them in the air and carry them forwards as they fly.

Birds in flight.

A Bird's Wings

A bird's wings are light and strong but flexible. They are strong enough to carry a bird's weight as well as some food and nesting materials. Inside the wings are bones and muscles. The wing muscles push and pull the bones so they act like levers and make the wing flap up and down. The shape of the wing is very important. It is curved so that the air above the wing flows more quickly than the air underneath. Fast flowing air has a lower pressure than slow moving air, so this helps lift the bird up as it flies.

Very small 'barbs' link together on the surface of a feather.

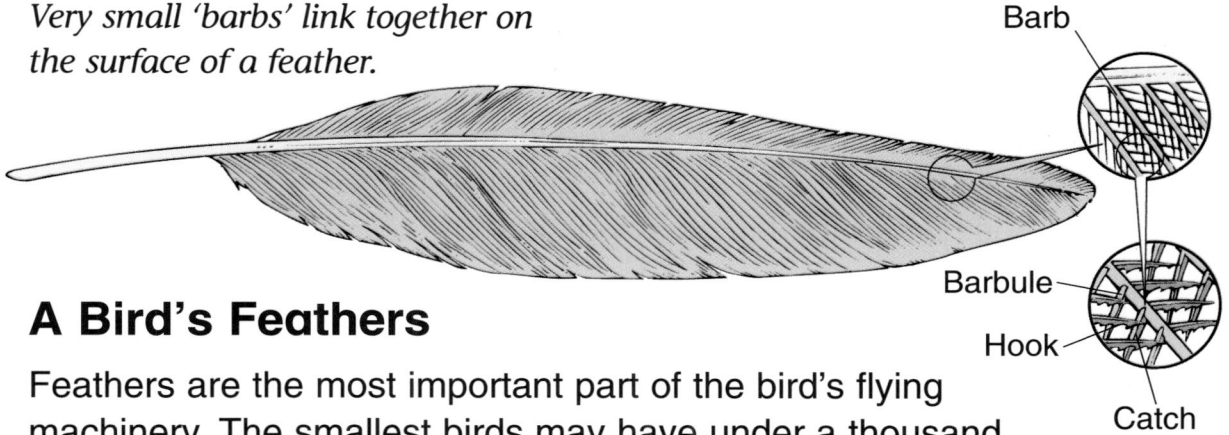

Barb

Barbule

Hook

Catch

A Bird's Feathers

Feathers are the most important part of the bird's flying machinery. The smallest birds may have under a thousand feathers, but big birds like swans may have over twenty-five thousand feathers. Feathers are made from a protein called **keratin**. Keratin makes them strong but flexible. The surface of a feather is made up from thousands of little barbs and barbules that hook up together. Feathers need to be kept smooth so the air flows over them, so birds preen them with their beaks. They bathe in water or dust to keep their feathers clean and free from lice and other insects.

The largest feathers help to steer the bird's flight.

Types of Feathers

There are four main types of feather that make up a bird's plumage. These are the body feathers, the down feathers and the tail and the wing feathers. The wing feathers are the most important for flying. On the outer part are the largest feathers. These give the bird most of its power. They can also be used to steer. They are usually thinner one side than the other. This helps them cut through the air. On the inner part of the wing are feathers that curve to help lift the bird in the air.

Feathers for Stabilising

Another group of feathers shape the wing into the body
to stop the bird being rocked around while it is flying.
At the top of the wing are special feathers which
spread open when the bird is flying slowly to
help it stay in the air.

*Feathers at top of
the wing can spread
open for stability.*

Feathers for Steering

Birds can also use their tail feathers for steering. They can use
the tail to give them extra lift when they are flying. When they
are landing, they can spread out the tail feathers to slow
themselves down, so the tail acts
like a brake.

*A bird's tail feathers
spread out for braking.*

The Shape of Birds' Wings

Birds' wings are shaped to help them fly in different ways. Birds that need to fly quickly to escape predators or catch their prey have broad rounded wings. Pigeons have strong wing muscles that help them take off and speed up quickly. Owls have fringes on their feathers that muffle the sound of their wings so that small animals don't hear them coming when they are hunting at night. Birds that migrate like swallows and swifts need to be able to fly a long way for long periods. They have curved, pointed wings that give them speed and help them stay in the air.

Different shaped wings for different ways of flying.

Flying Styles

Some birds can fly by gliding and soaring. Gliding means flying without flapping the wings. Soaring is gliding on warm air as it rises. Most birds can only glide for a few metres, but some can glide a long way, using the wind to help them stay high in the air. Gulls have thin pointed wings that help them glide. Large birds like eagles and buzzards glide and soar while they are hunting for food. Some birds can hover by beating their wings very quickly. Hummingbirds hover when they are feeding on nectar from flowers. Their wings can beat up to seventy times a second. Kestrels can hover while they hunt for small animals.

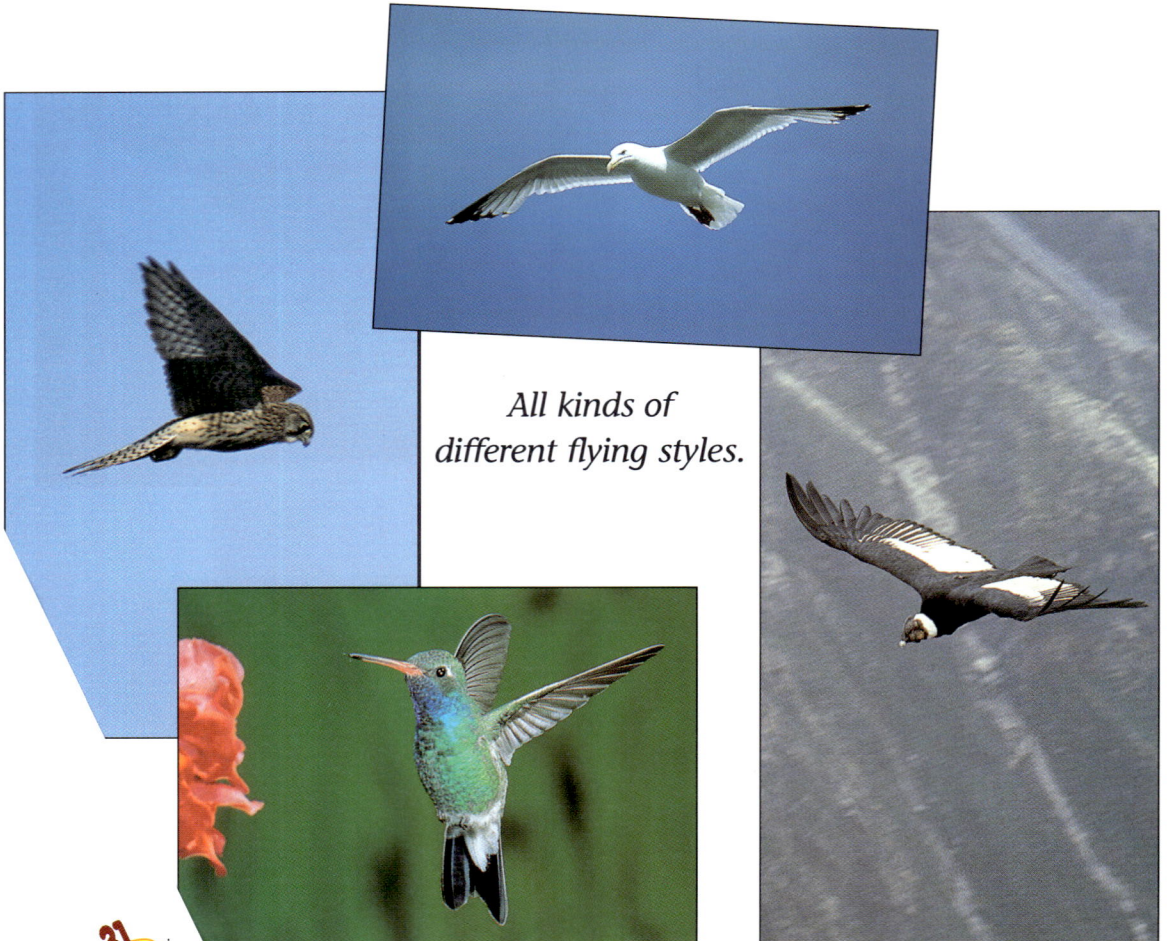

All kinds of different flying styles.